What Dragons Can't Deal With

Kim Lindeman

ISBN 978-1-7359617-1

Author's Note

I wrote this book in bits and pieces over a two-year period. It's not at all biographical, but it is the output that resulted from a difficult time in my life when I had no one to turn to for help except myself. For lack of a better idea, or any idea at all really, I began a daily routine of sitting in my car before work and writing using an app on my iPhone. Just a few minutes a day, spilling my thoughts on whatever came to mind. Sometimes what I was writing about was related to specific events or emotions I was processing and other times it was purely imaginative. Later, after work, I would go back and reread and edit them.

Anxiety, panic, fear and hopelessness were my most frequent visitors during this time, and I used writing to move through this period of darkness and finally return to, or at least find a window or two, of hope and peace.

I have heard many times that when you write a book, you are writing the book you need to read. I find it so interesting that although I never intended to write a book at all, I ended up with a collection of writings that were, and sometimes still are, what I need to read. I never aspired to be a writer or author when I started writing, but after going back to these writings many times over the years, I realized there could be someone else besides me out there who might find some value in them. It is my hope that you find something here that helps you in some way.

Dragons

some days I wish
I could be like a dragon

what dragons can't deal with
they roast

Table of Contents

How to Stop Panic Attacks?
and activities to improve mental health

1. **Follow internet tips from 21 year old psychology gurus like:**

   Never stare at yourself in the mirror
   This was far too tempting for me. I had not done this
   before, but once I read it, I found myself constantly
   stealing surreptitious eye locks with myself in every
   mirror, window, door and screen I passed. As if to
   dare myself to freeaaak out

   or transfigure into something awful,

   or just tempt whatever unknown outcome might
         occur, like maybe me thinking

   yes, you are a crazy bitch

2. **Music**
   but not Marilyn Manson, or Barney.

3. **Binaural beats**
   This is sketchy - piping different sounds into each ear
   to change your brain waves. Can be very effective,
   but risky when your waves are already a bit wonky.

   Tip: Make sure you're not also picking up noise from
   your crazy family or a baby monitor.

4. **Stand your panic down**
   yell at it!
   flip it off!

tell your panic to piss off!.

5. **Watch stand-up comics**
   and remember, they're crazy too -and successful!

6. **Drink**
   Baaad idea
   Even worse —drink in front of a mirror.

7. **Meditate**
   Good luck and keep trying. This one is certified but
   obviously hard to do when you're panicked.

8. **Eye shifts**
   When you feel panic rising-
   slam your eyes in an upward left direction
   do it again
   and again
   and again!

   this won't make you feel crazy
   -at all

   Advanced panickers only: do this in front
   of other people
   -or a mirror

9. **Identify all aspects of panic**
   bad physical feelings
   suffocating
   weird smells
   dizziness
   scary emotions
   heart pounding
   heart stopping
   feeling like you're being sucked into a hole

heart flopping around in your chest like a fish out of
water bouncing wetly in the dirt, eyes bulging,
gasping -yes that's it
stomach clenching
confusion
feelings of impending doom, death or disaster and
any other horrifying feeling that occurs for
no..fucking..reason.

Fun fact: Yes there's a smell sometimes

Note: There is no conceivable reason to do #9 except
masochism.

10. Hide it
Good luck trying.

11. Share it
Don't bother, no one gets it

12. Dirt Therapy and Grounding
dig in the dirt
sift the dirt
stand in the dirt
smell the dirt
lie in the dirt
kiss the dirt
eat dirt
be dirt

No comment

13. Shake /Wiggle —to release the Nasties

The Nasties don't want you to move - they like to be under covers in the dark.

14. Drive around
or just sit in an empty car
make interior covers
for all your car windows
so you can sit in your car
in parking lots
alone
in the heat
in the cold
alone
did I mention
alone

15. Devour the Internet
The cure must be in there somewhere-
IT MUST!!!

16. Stare at walls
or happy people——they hate that

17. Lie on the couch
roll over
try to breathe normally
pray
rage
cry
curse
get religion
get atheism
get Netflix

18. Snap your wrist with a rubber band
This will remind you that you're ok.
(whatever)

19. Recite crayon colors
Cognitive Behavioral Therapy I guess, but thinking about coloring children and the noise they make just made me angry.

20. Create elaborate mental fantasies
Like the one in Willy Wonka. This didn't work for me because mine only consisted of the creepy parts.

21. Go to the ER
when they say
there's nothing wrong with you
act like you're ok

22. Go home

23. Go back to step one

24. Start over

Dragons

Scent of Panic

a hazy memory of a scent
a smell inside my mind
reveals the time
when panic comes
to ring it's evil chime
the bells of hell
in crystal tones
ring clear for none to hear
except for me
just me— JUST ME
I hear it every time

Monster

all the petty little things
like slights
and fights
and arguments
suddenly cease
to matter

when you stare
into the eyes
of the monster

Unique

don't say you get it
you've been there before
or it's just like
what you went through

from what I can tell
each lesson in hell
is uniquely designed
just for you

Sunbeams

lying on the couch
her head falls to the side
as she peers listlessly
into the shadows

tiny sunbeams
float into the light
shining weakly
through the window
and she thinks

it's as if that dust
jumped off the blinds
and can't find a way
out of here either

Exposed

I scratch and dig
deeper and deeper
trying to find
the answers

and every new nugget
of knowledge I find
let's in
a little more light

to expose
the astonishing depth
of my stupidity

Sifting

why do you
keep going back
time and time again
with your half full bag
wasting hours
on hands and knees
sifting through rubble
for pieces you missed
hoping so hard
to finally find
that one last shard
that connects
all the parts
when it can never
-ever
be reassembled

Letting Go

the horse is dead
she has been
for quite some time now

I know this

I look at her lying
there on the ground
flies buzzing around her mouth and nose

I know she's gone
but I keep going back in my mind
pretending it's like before

and though of course
I know this

I can't stop poking
my foot in her ribs

I can't seem let her go

Holes

the dog that bit you
has long run off
but until the holes
have been cleaned
and dressed
the wound
will continue to fester

Lighthouse

who are you to tell me
there should be
no electronics
in the bedroom

you don't know
the bond I have
with the light
that glows
by my bed

some nights
it's all that stands
between me
and the silence
the cold
and the darkness
that creeps in
to smother me
swallow me whole

it's a beacon
it's all I have
to assure me
I'll find my way home

The Alien

when you feel like an alien
you don't fit in anywhere
and you can't just fly away
to a place where
everyone understands you

you don't have
a place of your own
a place that feels safe
like walking in
to the smells
of a mama's home cooking
where the screen door
slams shut behind you
enclosing you in
the warm welcoming
embrace of home

instead it feels
like someone's always yelling
and there's no cooking and
the slamming locks you out
and not in

when you're the alien
in your own home

My Pack

on days when memory
come closing in
and climbs up
to ride on my back

I know I can't shake her
or chase her away
so I drop her inside
of my pack

the one I've been dragging
around like a sack
full of groceries
I never unpack

it's filled to the brim
with things I collect
like ashes
smoke
and regret

she sits
face down in it
all day long
and looks up
only to nag me

she is heavy

the pack is heavy

the straps cut
into my skin

her hair is always
greasy and wet
and hangs down
over her face

I've never seen
what she looks like
I won't meet her
eye to eye

she's constantly talking
about how to stay safe
protect us
keep others away

don't make any plans
don't ever commit
just tell them
you'll try to make it

she says she gets me
she understands
she knows all
my secrets and sins

she wants me to learn from
the pain of my past
and make sure
that I never forget

Shield

it is not a mask
I hide behind
it is a shield I made
to protect me from people
who try to get
inside my mind

Callous

holding back feelings
may help you feel strong
but the callus that forms
just keeps getting thicker
and soon you feel nothing at all

Eyes

every eye constantly scans for
familiarity in movement

the way she reacts to a story
how he nods in agreement
a sudden intake of breath
in sync with your own
heard in a crowded room

we are all just looking
for reflections of ourselves
in a sea of beings
strangely similar
yet all so very different

seeking some kind of confirmation
that we are not alone

Spritz

spritz three times
the spray bottle makes that throaty sound
reverberating with each
squeeze squeeze squeeze

wipe it down
scrub it
wipe it
surfaces all sterile

thinking
thinking
spritz again
wipe everything down
thinking
processing

my mind
cannot be sanitized
but not for lack of trying

Transfixed

though I know it's futile
my heart cries out
for what's been squandered and lost

years that passed
in chaos

youth that dried up
and blew away
as time refused to stay still

and I unable to see
there was a way
to move forward

transfixed as I was
by the view
of the vanishing road

Small Talk

you're talking to me
looking at me
chattering and blathering
about everything yet nothing

my eyes point
in your direction
but inside I'm struggling
to appear normal
keep it under control

praying in desperation
that you can't see
or sense or hear
the pounding of my heart,
the clenching my teeth
the way my stomach and chest
twist together in a gordian knot.
that no amount of tugging will loosen

secretly wishing you would see
the war going on inside me
but you don't even notice

so I keep breathing
smile and nod
and say appropriate things
to the emptiness
that is you

Shards

she stood under the lamppost in the dark
staring up at the raindrops
coming straight at her
like tiny glass shards

feeling like one of them

flying free but knowing
that soon she too will
hit the ground and shatter

Empty Mirrors

she raced through life
grabbing strangers
by the shoulders
staring into their eyes
like empty mirrors
seeking some sign
looking for proof
that anyone could
really see her

Self help

I've blackened my own eyes
from the intensity of my stare
peering down deep
inside of myself
trying to see
what's probably glaringly
obvious
to everyone else

Trouble

sometimes I think
I am the errant child
of my frustrated soul
just here to cause
myself trouble

Relaxation

blur your eyes
bite your tongue
plug your ears with wax

block your nerves
numb your mind
now you can relax

Staying Inside

some storms are so strong
and make such a mess
that when the sun
finally comes out
I still won't go
back outside
I stay in and hide
gathering strength
until the next one arrives

Restraint

restraint they say
is what needs cultivating

develop some ropes
to hold myself back
from things not meant for me

but there's something
that loosens my grip
makes me fly off the rails

indulging in all sorts
of destructive delights
and then wondering
what's wrong with me

Faster

there was a time
when I wished so hard
for things to move a little faster

this too shall pass
they said

so I buried myself
in whatever I could
and prayed for it
to do so
quickly

forgetting that I
was not the only one
time was affecting

Listen

it had been so long
since she listened to herself
that the sound of her own voice
startled her back into silence

Silence

did you know
you can be in
a room full of people
self-destructing
right in plain sight

they can't see it

and you can't speak
not even squeak
to let them know
because you are
frozen in time
in a silent scream
that feels like it
won't ever stop

its amazing really
the things that can happen
right in front of your eyes

May

leaves fall
seasons must change
cold settles in
to clear the land
preparing the earth
for renewal

but death and decay
always disturb me
despite what they bring
come May

Inside

she never watched the snow anymore
never smelled the rain

never looked up at the moon anymore
never touched the earth

she never went outside anymore
and so inside
she died

The Dog

sometimes life
feels like you're
walking the dog
you begged your parents for

he's twice your size
and drags you down the road
while the neighbors laugh
behind curtains
as you leave chunks
of skin on the pavement
and you cry

but still-
you got the dog

Stopping Watches

she flattened the tips
of nails with a hammer
to make tiny screwdrivers
she used to take watches apart

day after day
watch after watch
trying to find a way
to make time stop
or slow down
or just figure out some trick
to interrupt the insidious tick
of the hand that
mocked her resistance

to the journey
she did not want to take

The Words Inside

the words are inside
but you are not ready
to think them
like a child who hides
from the consequence that
follows the deed

you busy yourself
with toys and distractions

never still long enough
to let the waters
of your mind settle
allowing what must be seen
to float to the surface

so it will roil and
churn in the deep
building in intensity

explosion
the only release

What's Real

I'm strange
and disconnected
and life seems
slightly out of focus

and sometimes I slap my cheeks
hard

just to make sure
I'm awake
   like -really awake

not just going along
upright but asleep

but then the slapping
feels unreal too

kind of like when
you die in a dream
and you know
it's not real
but it hurts anyway
and the pain
wakes you up

and for a moment

you know what's real

but by breakfast
you've forgotten

so you
just to go back
to the slapping

Oblivion's Blanket

in the darkest predawn
before the eyes crack
knowing creeps in
and worries the peace
which hides under
oblivion's blanket

The Deck

images of death that never fade
stack up like a pile of cards
all from the same deck

that's all they have in common
I don't need to turn them over
to see the faces
they are burned into my mind
each and every one

and I don't want to draw any more

how tall I wonder
will the stack get
before my card
is on top

Intentions

we try to do good
to be responsible

at least we say
don't kill anything

some even strive to follow
the greatest examples
from the finest minds
of all the history of mankind

but there's no hiding
no point denying
all of us
at one time or another
will lose our fucking minds

Balanced

you must find balance they say
I guess I will always be balanced
here on the edge of madness

Falling Stars

staring up at the stars
waiting for one to fall
was what she did
to convince herself
that anything mattered at all

Hours of Darkness

the days seem shorter
than they used to be
adding up to so many more
hours of darkness we use
to ponder
the things that live there

we get comfortable
there in the dark

our eyes adjust
and the light begins
to hurt

so we stay
and forget
the shadows we fear disappear
when you turn on the light

This Mess

some days I wish
I could blame
this mess on the devil

but then I think
he's probably not that creative

Anxiety

good morning my love
it was a horrible night
like it always is with you

you held me by the throat
all night long
and whispered terrible things

it's sick I know
we've been at this so long
I think I've become an addict

I know
I usually take you
everywhere with me
and keep you close by my side

but today
I head into danger
alone

I know it's your job
to protect me
from everything that I fear

I appreciate how hard you have tried
but I have to face some things
and say some words out loud
that you would never allow

even though I know

it's going to hurt me
so I'm just going to
leave you here this time
wrapped up
in my place on this bed

you know
I'll be back here
with you again
but someday this has to end

Dragons

Roast

Into the World

there's so much pain
in the birthing

howling and
wringing of hands
tearing at hair
ripping seams

the whole damn thing
threatening to come apart

as you bring your
real self
into the world

The Real You

if you opened
your eyes tomorrow
and promised to be
the real you

would the sun still feel
like it did yesterday
would everything
be the same

or would it seem
a little hotter
the wind
a little stronger
the smell of the earth
just a little bit sweeter

if you no longer
played the game

Breakdown

breakdowns don't always happen
because there's something
that needs to be fixed

some rides are just
not worth fixing

that's when it's best
to get out of the car

kick the fender
spit on the hood
and follow the road
back home

Breakthrough

sometimes the only difference
between a breakdown
and a breakthrough
is who gets to decide
what to call it

Shut up

go back to bed she said
it's no use
go back to bed and forget

but I have to take the kids to school
my report is due to today
and dinner...

go back to bed she said
it's pointless

what's the difference she said
where do you think you are all headed

all of you are dying
I'm dying
the world is dying
you're rats on a wheel
rolling towards the edge of a cliff
and there's no-

shut up
the one mouth said
to the other one in the mirror
I'm going to go out and live
and you're not
coming with me
today

Shadows

come
light a candle
let's take a trip down
to the darkened depths
of your uncharted heart

where the truth hides
and shadows reside
holding tight with
the ghosts of the past

then turn up that flame
burn up the names
and be free of
the darkness they cast

Exposure

she thought the blazing sun
would just magnify her fright
but she forgot most everything fades
with enough exposure to light

Housekeeping

I'm heading off
to the outer bands
of my dark and stormy mind
where I squirreled away
all of those things
I didn't want me to find

Shade

I suppose there's
 a little shade
in all of us

on the backside
of a whole lot of sun

I've been sitting
in darkness
a lot of late
it feels good
no cause for alarm

I write from this place
and it comforts my soul
to look into
the corners and see

what kinds of things
are lurking there
and why they are
hiding from me

Rubble

a poet mines their life
looking for nuggets to share

but truth be told
most of the gold
is found in the dirt
on the ground

in the rubble of things
we tried to forget
that insist on
hanging around

The Conqueror

I look in the mirror
squint
I can't understand
what I see
there are ashes in my hair
soot on my face
blood drips from a split
in my lip

there's honor
and strength
in a fight

but there was nothing
to conquer here

Growing Season

it's so cold out these days
and the sun seems to
have lost it's smile
and I...

I don't remember
what it feels like
to have one

but on days like these
it's kind of nice
to wrap myself up
in some warmth

lie down breathe shallow
go dormant and wait
for the growing season
to start

Hell

yes she said
hell is real
I know
I've been there before

but it's not exactly
what they say

because sometimes if you want
to leave bad enough
and you try
you can find a way out

Every Now and Then

if it's not too much trouble
as long as no one minds
every now and then
I get a little tired
    so...
I'm going to just go ahead
and put this light
under a bushel
until I'm ready
to get it out
again

Flick it

I don't want to write
another poem about
shadows and darkness

it's not what my soul is made of

my heart chases happiness
down the street
nipping the tires
and very often catching it

but here I am
once again
with it dripping
from my veins

so I pick up my pen
flick it twice
start the flow

I know better
than to try
to stop it

Frozen

in the silence
I sit and listen
to the erratic sound
of my frantically
beating heart

the rhythm is not even
the flow is broken
and every now and then
for a moment

just a moment

it stops

I like to imagine
it's a little reboot
a reset
to close all the
windows inside
that were frozen

Wounded

right now - today - for a while - I need silence
I just need to lie down here for a while
and curl myself around
my wounded parts
to protect them
and heal
and
someday
I'll tell you
what happened to me
but right now just leave me alone
I don't need your advice - I don't want to talk
but it would really be nice if you just kind of stayed
close by

Within My Reach

there is this need to light
to illuminate
to cast some warmth on something
within my reach

had I understood
I had only one ray
one beam
a single point of influence

I think I would have spent
a little more time
bringing the laser into focus

Pinch Yourself

a good hard slap
to the face
may wake you up

pinch yourself
if you think
it will help

whatever you do
it will never feel real

for the soul
can only move
so fast

Energy

energy is the same
no matter the source
gather strength
from your pain
let it build and ignite
at the first
sign of light
let it go

Attention

when you start
to pay attention

to where your attention goes

where you allow
your attention to go

suddenly becomes important

Eggshells

if you dance
on eggshells
long enough
they turn into
polished sand

Disconnected

in the disconnect
between real
and the things
you had planned
lie the roots
of deep unhappiness

sometimes things you
tried to grow may
have to be uprooted

Burned

there's nothing
you can't let go of
if the burn goes deep enough

Jesus

I only look for Jesus in the dark

stumbling around
with outstretched arms
trying to feel my way

stubbing my toes on pride
and other nasty things
that lie on the floor

things that make me
fall to my knees

which is probably right
where I need to be

Spark

all souls even those
lost in the dark
bear a spark of the light
they came from

Better Dreams

it seemed the universe gave her
all she had ever dreamed of
so she decided
it was time to start
dreaming better dreams

Crazy

take a close look
at what drives you crazy

first ask yourself
who's doing the driving

and second
why are you letting them
drive you anywhere

Zombies

put up some boundaries
carve out some room
for yourself

the zombies will scream
and tear at the fence
for a while

but if you stay strong
and don't open the gate
they'll find someone else
to feed on

A Brief History

I saw a shooting star tonight
and thought ...
when I'm gone that will be the expanse
of my life's meaning

just a flash in a vast whole
that left no meaning at all behind

the briefest of sparks that burned up in an instant

but...
I meant a lot to me

Hold On

I am learning how to let go

let go of
old things
new things
old hopes
old dreams
expectations of how things should be

I'm learning to hold on to me

Trapped

some days I wake up
and the air in my room
traps me right
where I lay

pulling me in
whispering spells
to keep
the world at bay

even the pillow
I'm curled around
seems to
want me to stay

those are the days
when I need to be still
and let the room
have its way

A Little Misty

I have hidden myself
away for so long
that sometimes I think
I will never be able
to touch my own cheek
or look into my eyes
without wondering

is this even me

or is it a shadow self
standing in for the one
who retreated
so far from this world
that moss has grown in her place

and all that is left
is a mound of her essence
here on the forest floor

and a shade who hovers near
telling those who ask
that she is fine
just feeling a little misty today

Knowing

at the river today
I walked the bank
looking for what
I don't know

I came upon a message
scratched in the sand
that read

you are here

and it was exactly
what I needed
to know

Your Mark

I am torn between a desire
to leave a mark on this world
and terror of
what it might look like

Questions

if I don't tell
or use in some way

what I have learned
from the grief
and the pain

then what purpose
did it serve

was it just an exercise
in tolerance
or patience
or endurance

on my way
to the day
of my death

More

people say
you will get through this
but there is nothing
to get through

this is simply
my life

and to get through
it is to get
to the end

and what good is there in
reaching for that

I experience this
all of it
and I am more
for having felt it

there is no good
or bad in life

just more

Baby bird

I know you're afraid
of having to leave
your safe and
comfortable shell

but as any baby
bird can tell you
breaking through
crawling out and
falling from the tree

is extremely scary
and painful

but once you're out
you'll never miss
the prison that
you came from

Accomplishments

and what did you
accomplish today he asked

I was brave
I showed up
I stood up for myself

and that was enough for one day

A Challenge

pain upon pain
can become
less torture
and more challenge

if that's how you chose
to view it

The Light Around Us

terrible terrible things happen
I know
it's falling all around us

but open your heart and
feel for the good
it's there if you
know how to look

it's there
it can heal
if enough
of us feel
for the light
and the good
that surrounds us

Almost Here

do not despair
and do not ever
become complacent

keep going
keep believing
for no matter where you are
and what you think right now
the end and the beginning
of something
is always almost here

Happy Endings

the world seems to
just want to hear
stories with happy endings
but endings are mixtures
of all sorts of things
like treasures and train wrecks
babies and breakdowns
deaths and exposed dirty laundry
sometimes the endings
we cherish the most
are the best
because something
is over

Endings

sometimes we think it's really the end
but it all just keeps on coming

the love the laughter
the grief and the tears
and everything in between

all these ridiculous
feelings we have
that swing to each extreme

despite our resistance
or how we pretend
what we love won't
move to the past

in the end even endings
themselves never end
because ends are the
seeds of beginnings

and nothing is meant to last

Still

it wasn't a dark
and stormy night
it was dark and silent
the kind of silence that
makes the sound
of your heart
too loud to bear

the kind of silence
that seeps into your bones
and sucks out any faith
you might have had
that there's anyone
out there who cares

the kind of lull
that makes you
long for a storm
ache for the fury
of the wind
and the pounding rain
the breathtaking violence
that banishes stillness
jolts you to life
and wakes up your
will to survive

Ascend

Cling

cling
and cling
and cling
and cling
to have it all close
keep control

but what if
just once

you let it all go

and learn
what you need
to be whole

Sprout

I know it must feel
like you've been around
for such a very long time

but please don't give up yet
don't throw it all out
you're just about
ready to sprout

Messages

be silent
and listen
to the sound
of your heart
for even when
it's breaking apart
there's something
it's trying to tell you

How

if you numb yourself
to the things
that cause you discomfort

blind yourself
to all that doesn't
look good

cover your ears
to drown out
the sounds
that alarm you

how will you hear
what your heart
is trying to say

how will you see
the things
it wants to reveal

how will you go
where your soul
is trying to guide you

if the clues on the map
are things
you won't let yourself feel

Broken

butterflies with broken wings
must crawl from here to there
but they leave the finest trails
of lovely glitter everywhere

Closed Doors

closed doors
may break your pace
but sometimes doors
that get slammed
in your face
are the perfect place
to begin
a brand new painting

Shame

what is your shame
what have you done
that you really wish you hadn't

did you lie
did you steal
envy someone
cheat on a test
love someone
hate someone
hurt someone

why is it shameful
who told you it was
somebody handed you that burden
and you slung it over your shoulder
like a child who carries a backpack
heavier than his small frame
adding more to it each day
until his spine starts to warp
under the weight

if it's over
then
drop that junk
throw it to the ground
walk away
and don't ever -ever look back

Courage to Break

if tears make us weak
its done in the keeping

for true strength comes
from having the
courage to break
and allow them to flow

Wound Up

sometimes I get myself
wound up so tight
a thorough unraveling
is all that feels right

Grooved

the strongest hearts
don't break in half
it's really just pain
from life's
carving knife
making grooves
deep enough
for rivers of love
to keep flowing

Cracks

every time
they beat you down
with every single blow

the cracks they make
inside your soul
will never even show

but though they
cannot see it now
the thing they
do not know

is how each crack
gets filled with
steel that hardens
as you to grow

Progress

all these little steps I take
don't feel like they're
getting me anywhere

half steps side steps
baby steps
what ever it takes

I keep my eyes on my feet
and cheer them on
make sure they agree
to keep moving

once in a while
I raise my eyes
to see if I've made any progress

and the mountains still
look so far away
just like they do everyday

and the distance from here
to where I know I must go
is impossibly far and depressing

but sometimes I notice
the buildings have changed
or I'm in a new part of town

and looking back at those faces
receding into the distance

of people who said
I should stay in my place
is a good way
to measure my progress

Down

once I fell down
into the depths
of the place
I had tried to avoid

when I arrived
I was really surprised
to find everything
I had been missing

Within

when you can't find the way out
take a breath
look around
and find something to work on
within

Solitude

I sink into solitude
like a hot steaming bath
where I am perfectly willing to drown

White Space

cars whine a lonesome song
far off in the dusk
on the highway

clattering blinds
caught in a breeze
rattle a staccato rhythm

sunbeams float and swirl
in the slowly dying light
a few get pulled into the dark
drawn into the depth
of my silent breath

all these things
I used to call boredom
now feel
a lot like peace

Calling

there's a place in the wild
where the wind and the breath
are all the mind has to deal with
where whispery threads
of beckoning calls
cry out to the
souls of all wanderers

A Form of Resistance

I don't think I needed
to learn how to swim

it's kind of
a form of resistance

what I needed to learn
was how to just sink
without fearing to drown
in the stillness

Strange

we are all incredibly odd
and a little afraid to show it

but it's in sharing our weirdness
the connections we make
become so alive and amazing

so spread your weird
all over the place and ignore
when they call you crazy

Enveloped

if you sit in darkness
long enough

one puff
of fresh air
will choke you

one ray of sunlight
through a crack
in the wall

is enough
to nearly
blind you

fully enveloped
the darkness can feel
like a hole
you will never
crawl out of

but when something
gets through
even a spark

the beauty
is stark
and the light

illuminates
the shadows

Thanks

thank you for panic
thank you for pain

thanks for the anguish
that drove me insane

thank you for ledges
I almost fell off

for all of those thoughts
that I couldn't turn off

thank you for all of it
every last thing
that gave me
the strength and the
faith I would need

Reassembled

if I could take
your shattered world
and put it back together
exactly like it was at the start

I would never do it
because the way
you reassembled yourself
is a masterful work of art

Disaster

being whole again
doesn't mean
you're the same as before

after the disaster
you get to pick up
the pieces you like the most
and leave all the rest
on the ground

Resistance

if I could go back
and start over again
I'd do it again in an instant

but this time I'd do it
expecting some pain
and I'd do it
without the resistance

Riches

she dreamed not of romance
riches or glory
but open skies and
empty days of silence
filled only by
the soothing sound
of her own breath

Tending

a tiny seed
of self loathing
may be there
within us all

but how you tend to
the soil of your soul
can kill it or
cause it to grow

Things That Break

some things that break
will never heal
and perhaps
it's better that way

if it meant enough
to hurt that much
it must have been
really important

and after enough
time has passed
and we can stand
to sit with the pain

it starts to sink in
it's ever so thin
like a newly formed
layer of skin

still tender to touch
fragile at first
but strengthening over time

the process is raw
painful for sure
but I think that's
how we become.

Scar Tissue

some things in youth
are lost
in the course
of growing

baby teeth don't grow back
when you lose them
and neither does virginity

or the skin
that you shed
when you fall down
over
and over
and over
ripping off
the same old scab
20 or 30 times
until finally
you learn the lesson

it was never
about trying to get back
things you lose
as you're learning

the point
is the strength
of the scar tissue

Finish Line

sometimes in the end
all you can do is
stumble
and trip
and fall
across the finish line
depleted
exhausted
and stripped
of your pride

but there
on the ground
gasping for breath
you may find
the most powerful
victory

Clarity

the answers are there
you just can't see them
from here

walk away
and keep on walking
till you're
far enough out
to look back

across the distance
in space and time
you may find the
clarity you lack

Better or Worse

beware the thought
it can't get
any worse

that hole
can always get bigger

it's bottomless
and stretching
to make some room
for more of your
misplaced treasures

but the same is true
of the opposite thought
that things couldn't
get any better

Source of Light

the air surrounding a candle
is always the blackest black
like looking out a window at night
when you yourself
are the source of light
it's hard to see into the dark

On My Knees

when I get down
on these carpet worn knees
and try to pray
these days

I don't beg for forgiveness
or what I want day to day
I don't even ask
for strength

I don't ask for patience
or help finding my way
I don't even care
where I'm going

I've whispered all that
in the dead of the night
to tear soaked pillows
when nothing felt right
and picked it back up
in the morning

starting again
right where we left off
and it's never
done any good

so when I drop to my knees
to say something these days
I don't use a script
I'm not asking

I forgive all the people
I forgive the whole world
I love everyone
and I'm sorry

but that doesn't
help me to swallow this life
or help get my feet moving forward

what I'm trying to say is
what really works
is to leave it in
capable hands

get out of the way
and pray for the grace
to accept
what I don't understand

The Plunge

the initial shock
stopped her heart
darkness overcame

breathless and silent
hopeless and lost
blackness pulling her down

there on the bottom
struggling to breathe
fighting against the weight

she suddenly stopped
surrender complete
and gracefully rose
to the top

Salted Caramel

I like my salted caramel
bacon covered doughnut life

it makes no sense
and it's not what
I would have chosen

but the tastes is so strange
that it sticks to the tongue
and gives me a lot
to think on

Stuff and Nonsense

the skeptics say
there is no magic
that it's all just
stuff and nonsense

but I know magic
her sister mystery
and her brother music

I know they're real
they do exist
but they never show up uninvited

In You

I'm your mother
your daughter
your most precious babe
I am 80 and 50 and 12

the hands of time
do not wrap around me
for I am
outside of this realm

I'm timeless
and homeless
I live in the wind
I exist in each
breath that you take

there is nothing
and nowhere
that I don't move through

I am love
and I'm here inside you

39443809R00090